MATH YOU WILL ACTUALLY USE™

# USING MATH IN FASHION

CHRISTY MIHALY

rosen publishing's
rosen central®
NEW YORK

*To E. M. and A. M., who love math, fashion, and books, too*

Published in 2018 by The Rosen Publishing Group, Inc.
29 East 21st Street, New York, NY 10010



First Edition



**Library of Congress Cataloging-in-Publication Data**

Names: Mihaly, Christy.
Title: Using math in fashion / Christy Mihaly.
Description: New York : Rosen Publishing, 2018 | Series: Math you will actually use | Includes bibliographical references and index.
Identifiers: ISBN 9781499438604 (pbk.) | ISBN 9781499438628 (library bound) | ISBN 9781499438611 (6 pack)
Subjects: LCSH: Fashion—Mathematics—Juvenile literature.
Classification: LCC TT497.M54 2018 | DDC 746.9'20151—dc23

*Manufactured in the United States of America*

| METRIC CONVERSION CHART | |
|---|---|
| 1 inch = 2.54 centimeters; 25.4 millimeters | 1 cup = 250 milliliters |
| 1 foot = 30.48 centimeters | 1 ounce = 28 grams |
| 1 yard = .914 meters | 1 fluid ounce = 30 milliliters |
| 1 square foot = .093 square meters | 1 teaspoon = 5 milliliters |
| 1 square mile = 2.59 square kilometers | 1 tablespoon = 15 milliliters |
| 1 ton = .907 metric tons | 1 quart = .946 liters |
| 1 pound = 454 grams | 355 degrees Fahrenheit = 180 degrees Celsius |
| 1 mile = 1.609 kilometers | |

# CONTENTS

INTRODUCTION.....4

**CHAPTER 1**
FASHION CENTS (AND DOLLARS).....6

**CHAPTER 2**
THE PERFECT FIT.....10

**CHAPTER 3**
SKETCH IT IN STYLE: CREATING YOUR OWN LOOK.....15

**CHAPTER 4**
MAKE YOUR OWN.....21

**CHAPTER 5**
GOING PRO WITH A PROTOTYPE.....27

**CHAPTER 6**
MAKING MONEY IN THE FASHION BUSINESS: COSTS, PRICES, AND PROFIT.....32

ANSWERS.....36

GLOSSARY.....39

FOR MORE INFORMATION.....41

FOR FURTHER READING.....43

BIBLIOGRAPHY.....44

INDEX.....46

# INTRODUCTION

You probably don't solve long division problems while watching *Project Runway,* and you may think multiplication tables aren't relevant to the clothes you're wearing. But whether you're shopping for bargains on boots, creating a cool costume, or planning a career in fashion design, math can make for some smooth styling. It turns out that you can't have fashion without math!

Fashion designers use math every day. They use concepts from geometry, such as proportions and volume, in creating new designs. They need to make accurate measurements in order to size their clothing correctly. Designers use ratios when translating fashion sketches into reality. If they're selling their work or running a fashion business, they use mathematical analysis to set the prices of their products. And math helps them count how much money they're making—and identify when they need to cut costs or raise prices.

Of course, you don't have to be a professional designer to enjoy fashion. Maybe you're just interested in making clothes for yourself. Sewing is a creative and money-saving hobby that lets you make the clothing you want to wear. You'll find that your math skills come in handy at the sewing machine. You'll need to know how to measure accurately to select the right pattern size, determine how much fabric you need, and then make alterations as needed. In sewing, mere fractions of an inch can make a big difference.

The woman on the right is taking careful, accurate measurements with a measuring tape. Measuring is an important step in creating properly fitted fashions.

On the other hand, maybe your main interest in fashion is wearing it! If so, you'll still find that numbers matter. Measuring helps you know what size to buy. Math helps you calculate what clothing purchases are within your budget, too. When you're looking at sales prices on garments, you need math to compute how much money you'll save with different discounts. This is math you will actually use.

CHAPTER 1

# FASHION CENTS (AND DOLLARS)

Whether you're looking for the latest fashion in shoes or stocking up on basics for going back to school, shopping for clothes means counting out the cash. Math will help you figure out whether those fashion finds are within your budget. You'll need to know your dollars and cents. And when you're hitting the sales, it pays to understand percentages, too.

A 40 percent discount offers a large amount of savings. These shoppers can calculate the exact price they'd pay for these garments with math.

## BUDGET BUYS AND FASHION FINDS

Most people don't have unlimited money to spend on fashion. Instead, they stick to a clothing budget, or a specific amount of money available to spend on clothes. If your budget is limited, you'll want to spend your money wisely. You can compare clothing prices by visiting several stores and checking the prices you'd pay to buy online. You may find discounts or special sales.

## FASHION FOR THE ENVIRONMENT

You can save money on clothes while helping the environment. Consider these ways to cut down on waste and reduce your carbon footprint (you'll probably think of more):

*Resell:* Take clothing you've outgrown or are tired of wearing to a resale store. Selling your used clothes could earn you cash or store credit. (Check with a parent or guardian first.)

*Recycle:* Have a clothing swap with friends. That's when you all clean out your closets and meet up. You bring the clothes you no longer want, check out your friends' discards, and pick what you like. With luck, everyone heads home with some fresh wardrobe additions.

These fashion-conscious friends are participating in a clothing swap at one of their homes. It's a fun way for them to clear out clutter and update their wardrobes.

For example, you might see a store advertising 30 percent (also written as 30%) off original prices. You need to know that 30 percent means 30 per 100, or 30 out of 100. That's the same as $^{30}/_{100}$, or 0.30. If you take the original price and multiply it by 0.30, you get the amount of the discount, or price reduction.

What if you see a sign announcing a 50 percent markdown? That's easier to calculate. Fifty percent, or $^{50}/_{100}$, can be reduced to $^{1}/_{2}$. Just divide the original price by two. That's half off—a pretty good deal.

You can also save money by checking out secondhand shops. Goodwill and other resale shops or thrift stores sell items that have been previously owned. They offer clothes at good discounts, sometimes as much as 80 percent lower than at retail outlets. In 2013, Deal News relied on industry surveys to estimate that Americans had saved a total of about $4 billion by buying clothing at thrift stores the prior year. Thrift stores often offer a range of new and old styles and one-of-a-kind items. You have to shop carefully, though, because the quality and prices will vary.

## SHOPPING ONLINE

If you're a smart shopper, buying on the Internet can save you money. Here are some words of wisdom for the web.

*Ask an adult.* You'll probably need to borrow an adult's credit or debit card for an online purchase. Talk with that adult about which websites are safe and whether buying an item online is cheaper than going to a store. Does the card company charge fees or interest on purchases? If so, are you still saving money?

*Consider quality.* Are there online complaints about the seller

## TRY IT YOURSELF

Sam has a budget of $50.00 for new clothes. He needs a shirt and jeans.

At Jeans for Beans, Sam's favorite store, jeans normally cost $40.00. Today, Sam finds a pair in his size on a rack labeled "25% off."

Shirts are usually $22.50, but Sam sees two shelves of shirts with sales. On the first shelf, the sign says, "Buy one, get one HALF PRICE." On the second shelf, the discount reads, "$5 off."

1a. How much would a pair of jeans on the sales rack cost? How much money would Sam have left?

1b. Can he buy a shirt with what remains?

1c. If he buys a shirt, how much is left over?

or product you're considering? If an item falls apart, it's not a good deal! What's the average rating? If the site uses a five-star system, it's usually best to stick with items that have an average of four stars or more. You could think of four out of five as equivalent to $^4/_5$, or 80 percent.

*Watch for hidden costs.* Don't click "buy" until you've reviewed shipping costs and other charges that may be added to your order. Some sites offer free shipping if you make a minimum purchase. Consider whether it's worth buying more items to get free shipping. If you pay for shipping, is it still a good value?

*Review return policies.* Return policies vary. No matter how low the price is, it's a bad deal if you don't like it and can't return it.

CHAPTER 2

# THE PERFECT FIT

You're looking for clothes that look good. So you'll want them to fit. Finding the right fit starts with measuring. Sizing charts can help. But to get the perfect size, you'll usually have to try things on and sometimes make alterations.

## WHAT SIZE ARE YOU?

While shopping, you'll notice that clothing manufacturers use different sizing systems. You could determine your size by going into a store and trying on many different sizes, one after another. This can take a lot of time!

Another method is to measure. The best way is to use a measuring tape, which is a long, flexible ruler marked with inches and/or centimeters. Generally, you'll measure to the nearest quarter inch.

Let's use pants as an example. To find out your pants size, you'll measure your waist and your inseam, or the inside of your leg. Measure the narrowest part of your waist—without sucking in your stomach! Make sure you're measuring from zero to whatever the measurement is, and hold the tape snug but not too tight around your waist. Look at the number that the end of the tape hits as you hold it. To measure your inseam, you could measure the inside leg seam of a pair of pants that fit the way you like. Otherwise, hold the tape at the top of the inside of your leg while standing and measure straight to the floor.

Once you have your measurements, consult the clothing manufacturer's size chart to see which size you're closest to. For example, Jordan measured his waist at 24 inches (in) and his inseam at 26 3/4 inches. He consults the size chart at the bottom of this page.

Jordan isn't an exact match. Many people aren't! You'll still need to try on the clothes to see how they fit. But based on his measurements, Jordan could probably save time by trying on size 11 slim pants to start.

| Boys' Jeans Sizes | Waist (in) | Inseam (in) |
|---|---|---|
| 10 slim | 23 | 25 |
| 10 regular | 25 | 25 |
| 11 slim | 23 1/2 | 27 1/2 |
| 11 regular | 25 1/2 | 27 1/2 |

| MEN SHIRT SIZE (cm) | | | | | | | |
|---|---|---|---|---|---|---|---|
| SIZE | XS | S | M | L | XL | XXL | 3XL |
| Collar | 37 | 38 | 39 | 40 | 41 | 42 | 43 |
| Chest | 98 | 102 | 106 | 110 | 114 | 118 | 122 |
| Length | 75 | 77 | 77 | 79 | 79 | 81 | 81 |
| Sleeve | 58 | 59 | 60 | 61 | 62 | 63 | 64 |
| Cross Shoulder | 46 | 47 | 48 | 49 | 50 | 51.5 | 53 |

Men's shirts are often sized by collar, sleeve, and chest measurements. This chart of men's shirt sizes shows shirt dimensions in centimeters.

## ALTERATIONS: MEASURE TWICE AND CUT ONCE

Most human bodies don't exactly match the sizes of the clothes sold in stores. That means the clothes you buy don't always fit perfectly, and you may need to make some alterations. Sometimes this can be done in the store. Otherwise you, or a friend or family member, could do it at home. Remember that it's easier to adjust a garment that's too big, rather than too small.

Maybe you bought some pants on sale, and they're a little too long. You could adjust the hem to make them fit just right. Start by measuring. Suppose your pants are 1 $^1/_2$ inches too long. Turn the pant leg inside out. Measure 1 $^1/_2$ inches from the bottom and mark the place with a piece of chalk or pencil. Do this at spots all the way around both pant legs. Then fold the bottom of the pants up along the marks and secure the hem with pins. Check to make

## TRY IT YOURSELF

Ame's older cousin gave her a dress she had outgrown. Ame loves the dress but it's too long for her. From the waist to the hem, the dress now measures 17 in.

Ame measured from her waist to the point where she wants the hem of the dress to fall. She decided she'd like the dress to measure 14 ½ in from the waist to the finished hem.

2a. How much should Ame cut off of the dress?

2b. Ame wants to shorten the dress by folding under a hem of 1 ¼ in all the way around the bottom of the dress. She will first cut off the excess fabric around the bottom, leaving just enough for her hem. How much fabric should Ame cut off?

sure you have 1 ½ inches of fabric folded under on the inside of the garment. Then press the fabric flat and sew it under.

*Emergency alteration*: Don't have a needle and thread handy? In a pinch, you can use duct tape, safety pins, or even staples to temporarily hold up a drooping hem. Don't forget to sew it up later!

# DECODING THE DIMENSIONS

You'll run into different sizing systems while clothes shopping. There are boys' sizes, girls' sizes, junior sizes, and adult sizes. Some clothes come in petite and others in plus size. Different countries use different systems, too.

| US /Canada | Europe |
| --- | --- |
| 2 | 32 |
| 4 | 34 |
| 6 | 36 |
| 8 | 38 |

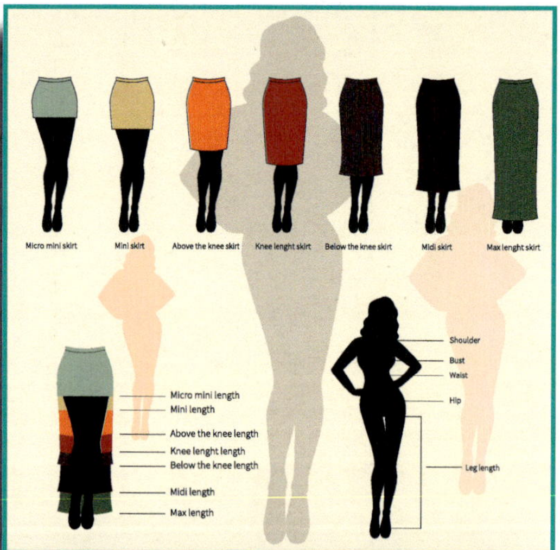


A diagram like this one can help you determine where the hem of a skirt will fall before you try it on. Different manufacturers may use different terminology.

Some clothes sold in the United States and Canada use European sizes, for instance. The good news is that once you know your size in one system, you can consult a conversion chart to find your corresponding size in another system. This chart shows how to convert from the US/Canadian women's size to a European size.

Thus if Ming usually wears an American size 4, she'll look for a size 34 in European sizes.

It can be especially challenging to order the right size when you shop online. But knowing your measurements can help here, too. Check the online size charts. Then search the website for the dimensions of the item you want to buy. For example, if you're interested in a skirt, look for a statement of its length on the website. If you'd like a skirt that's 18 inches long and you're looking at a skirt with a listed length of 15 ½ inches, it's shorter than you want. If it's too long, on the other hand, you might order it anyway and plan to shorten it.

CHAPTER 3

# Sketch It in Style: Creating Your Own Look

You may think fashion design is all about the art. But here's the thing: to be a designer, you don't need to be a great artist. However, it helps to know math! For instance, geometry comes in handy when you first sketch your ideas and again when you turn those two-dimensional designs into three-dimensional (3D) reality.

## GIVE SHAPE TO YOUR IDEAS WITH GEOMETRY

A design usually starts with a drawing. When making a rough sketch, you can outline your design with basic geometric shapes. For example, a series of rectangles makes the shape of a jacket: bigger rectangles for the body of the jacket and skinnier rectangles for the sleeves. If you think you

Geometric shapes such as these, alone or in combination, form the basis for many fashion designs. Experimenting with different shapes can help to create a new look.

can't draw, try cutting rectangles, triangles, ovals, and other shapes out of colored paper. Then lay the cutout shapes onto white paper to make your design. For example, you could use triangles for a skirt and create a hat design with a circle and a square. You can experiment with shapes.

Of course, the design doesn't end with a flat drawing. A square or rectangular piece of paper or fabric has only two dimensions: length and width. You can calculate the area $(A)$ taken up by a rectangle by measuring the length $(L)$ and the width $(W)$. The formula for a rectangle's area is:

$A = L \cdot W$

In order to turn a two-dimensional sketch into wearable clothing, you'll have to add a third dimension, height $(H)$. Height is sometimes called depth. Since a square is a two-dimensional shape with equal length and width, assembling six squares of the same size makes a cube with equal length, width, and height. A 3D object has volume, meaning it takes up space. The formula for the volume $(V)$ of a cube is:

$V = L \cdot W \cdot H$

As squares can be combined to make a cube, flat pieces of fabric can be joined together to construct three-dimensional garments.

## LEONARDO DA VINCI

Leonardo da Vinci, the great artist and scientist of the Italian Renaissance, spent years studying various proportions, or size relationships, that he observed in nature. He was particularly fascinated with the proportions of the human body. You may have seen his famous sketch of a human figure inside of a circle and a square. He completed this sketch, popularly called "The Vitruvian Man," around 1490.

In this sketch, Leonardo blended art and geometry. He showed the man's arms and legs in different positions. The feet and fingers of the man exactly reach the outlines of the geometrical figures. Leonardo's notes on the diagram list various relationships between the different measurements of the human figure. For example, he states that the man's height equals the distance between the fingertips of his outstretched arms.

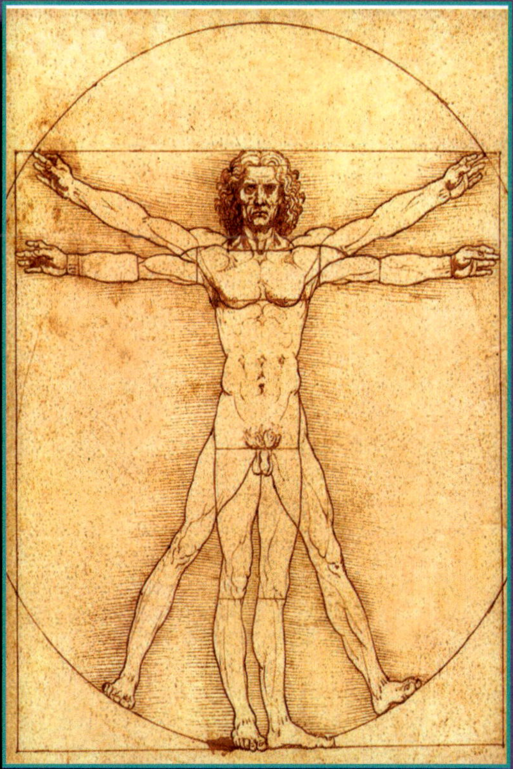

Da Vinci's Vetruvian Man demonstrates the geometrical proportions of the human body. Proportions are a basic starting point for designing clothing.

Here's a way to think about volume in fashion. Say the objective is to make a tote bag. Cut out a square front fabric panel and decorate it, perhaps with a tree design. Make a back panel that is the same size as the front. Sew these two pieces together along the bottom and two sides and add handles at the top.

But if you wanted a container that could hold all of your notebooks, your jacket, and your bicycle helmet, you'd need a bag with greater volume. You'd need to think in three dimensions to make a tote bag that's shaped more like an open box, or rectangular prism. A rectangular prism is a three-dimensional object with six faces

Both of these tote bags are handy. They each hold many objects because their depth gives them a great carrying capacity.

## TRY IT YOURSELF

Jared is making a book bag for Bubbe, his grandmother. It needs to be large enough to carry the three books Bubbe brings home each week from the library. Jared gets some tough fabric, thread, and sharp scissors.

Jared wants a boxy bag shaped like a paper shopping bag, rather than one that's flat like an envelope. He'll cut a piece for the front of the bag, a piece for the back, and two handles. To give the bag the shape he wants, he'll also include separate pieces for the bottom and the sides.

Jared wants the front and back of the bag to be 14 inches long and 12 inches wide. He measures Bubbe's stack of books. It's 3 ½ inches high. He decides the bag should be 4 inches deep so the books will fit. He designs a bag with a bottom measuring 4 inches by 12 inches. He'll sew in two side panels between the front and the back. On the finished bag, the side panels are each 4 inches by 14 inches.

3a. What is the volume of Jared's bag?

that are all rectangles. And since a square is a type of rectangle, a cube is also a rectangular prism. It follows that the volume of a rectangular prism (like that of a cube) is: $V = L \cdot W \cdot H$. If the measurement of each dimension is in inches, the volume will be expressed in cubic inches ($in^3$). (A cubic inch is the volume of a cube measuring 1 inch for each dimension.)

# MATH MATTERS

Some high-fashion designs are wild and wacky—and that's part of their appeal. But for a style to become really popular, people have to think it looks fabulous. It should be attractive on a real person, too, not just a mannequin.

A design's sense of balance affects how people respond to it. Artists and architects strive for beauty by creating balanced proportions in their paintings, sculptures, and buildings. The relationships between the width, length, and height of a particular room or building affect how a person feels entering it. Architects and artists use mathematics to create balance and beauty.

Fashion designers also use these principles in their work. They may experiment with different proportions in creating original styles. A designer might combine elements such as tight pants and a billowy jacket or a long, full skirt with a tailored vest to see how these shapes balance one another. In fashion design, it's important to consider the proportions of the human body, too. These elements affect the fit, as well as the appearance, of an outfit. Thoughtfully designed clothing can help the wearers look—and feel—their best.

CHAPTER 4

# MAKE YOUR OWN

If you're ready to join the DIY (do-it-yourself) crowd and create your own styles, congratulations! You'll need a working knowledge of inches, feet, and yards. With a measuring tape and a few more tools of the trade, you'll be ready to go.

## FASHION CONVERSIONS

In fashion there are several different kinds of conversion. Sometimes it's converting measurements from the metric system to the United States customary system. For example, the chart provided in the beginning of this book shows that 1 inch equals 2.54 centimeters (cm). So to convert from inches to centimeters, multiply by 2.54. Other times, you might consult a size conversion chart to go from one clothing system to another, such as from American to European sizes.

This measuring tape is marked with both metric and US customary measurements. These markings aid in converting between the two systems.

When sewing your own designs, you'll encounter another type of conversion: converting different types of units within a single measurement system. Much of the fashion industry still uses the United States customary system of inches, feet, and yards. You'll often need to convert between these different units when sewing. You can easily do this if you know the relationships between the different measurements.

For example, 1 foot (ft) contains 12 inches. That means if you need 4 feet of trim to decorate a jacket, it's the same as saying you need 48 inches. This is because $4 \cdot 12$ in = 48 in.

It is a little more complicated to measure the amount of fabric required to make a garment. Here, you'll be looking at square area rather than length. You'll use the formula $A = L \cdot W$.

The area of fabric you need for a project could be measured in terms of square feet ($ft^2$) or square yards ($yard^2$). Convert between square feet and square yards by remembering that 1 square foot is the area of a square measuring 1 ft on each side, while a square yard measures 1 yard by 1 yard. Don't forget that 1 yard = 3 feet. That means that 1 $yard^2$ measures 3 feet by 3 feet. Multiply 3 ft • 3 ft to determine that there are 9 $ft^2$ in 1 $yard^2$.

## A COMMERCIAL SEWING PATTERN CALCULATES CONVERSIONS

Commercially available clothing patterns allow you to sew a range of fashions at home. You'll find patterns online and in fabric stores. A pattern

With a commercial pattern, pin the printed pattern to the fabric. Then cut the shapes from the fabric and follow the directions to sew them together.

comes in a package that includes papers printed with the outlines of each piece of fabric to cut out, a list of other materials you'll need, and step-by-step directions. Here's how it works:

*Select your style.* Browse photos and sketches from pattern collections. Choose one you like. (It's best to start with a simple one.)

*Find your size.* Compare your body measurements against the company's size chart.

*Gather supplies and materials.* The pattern directions list the necessary materials, such as thread and buttons.

*Measure and purchase fabric.* Your pattern will include pattern pieces in the shapes needed to construct your garment. The pattern will specify how much fabric to buy. For example, you may need 18 $ft^2$ of fabric to cut out your pattern pieces. Fabric comes in different widths. It's usually sold by the yard. Most commercial patterns include a chart indicating the amount of fabric required for each size of the garment. The chart specifies how long a piece of fabric you'll need, depending on whether the fabric is sold in a 45-inch width or a 60-inch width. The pattern maker makes the calculations to help you determine how many yards of fabric you'll need.

*Follow directions.* A sewing pattern includes instructions for sewing the garment. You'll start by laying out the pattern pieces on the fabric by following a diagram provided with the pattern. It's like a geometric puzzle. You'll pin the pieces into position and cut the fabric around the outlines of the pattern pieces to produce the pieces of your garment. Then follow the steps to sew the pieces together.

# CONVERT THAT OLD T-SHIRT INTO A BRIGHT NEW FASHION STATEMENT!

Maybe you haven't picked up a needle and thread before. No problem. You can ease into making your own clothes with a different kind of conversion: converting an old t-shirt into a new garment with a stitch-free project.

If the sleeve of your favorite t-shirt is ripped or stained, consider making it into a tank. Just cut off the sleeves. But don't throw them away! You can turn those sleeves into headbands. Take the sleeve (bigger sleeves work better) and trim it into a band 2 to 4 inches wide. You can glue on a flower or other decoration if you want. For a fancier project, cut several old, unwanted t-shirts into long strips of fabric and then braid the long pieces together to make a belt or bracelet.

The possibilities expand when you start sewing. You can transform old t-shirts into rugs, skirts, or hats. As an example, here's an easy way to create a scarf from several different-colored t-shirts.

## TRY IT YOURSELF

Sondra needs 30 $ft^2$ of fabric to sew a dress. She finds a style she likes. It comes in a 60-inch width, and its length is 1 yard.

4a. How many yards of fabric will Sondra need to purchase in order to have 30 $ft^2$ of fabric?

The thread in this photo has been used to make a variety of colorful bracelets. Using recycled materials like t-shirts can create designs that are just as creative.

Measure and cut squares of fabric, 6 inches by 6 inches, from the shirts. Then stitch those squares together in a line. How many squares would you need for a 5-foot scarf? Because 1 foot is 12 inches, multiplying 12 inches by 5 tells you your scarf will be 60 inches long. Dividing 60 inches, the length of the scarf, into 6 inches, the length of one fabric square, gives you 10. You'll need 10 of your fabric squares (disregarding the amount needed for the seams between the squares). Which old t-shirts will you be converting into your new favorite scarf?

CHAPTER 5

# Going Pro with a Prototype

Professional fashion designers experience the thrill of seeing their ideas come to life on the runway. To make that happen, fashion pros need to know about manufacturing and math, as well as beauty and design. Computers and other tools help them do their work, but designers need a solid appreciation of math concepts, including ratios and scale.

## PROTOTYPES: SCALING IT UP

A fashion designer starts by sketching an idea for a new outfit on paper or a computer. It often takes many drafts to get it just right. Once the design is polished and ready, it becomes the basis for constructing a sample garment, or prototype.

The designer outlines the sizes and shapes of all the pieces of fabric that will be combined to make the outfit. There's no preprinted pattern in this scenario! The designer also selects the type and color of fabric for the prototype. Then the pieces are assembled into a three-dimensional sample.

After the prototype is constructed, the designer reviews it. Does the garment drape the way it's supposed to on a mannequin or model? Do the length and the proportions seem right? The designer may make adjustments to improve the fit and appearance. Perhaps the collar should be 3 $1/2$ inches wide instead of 4 $1/4$ inches. Maybe the sleeves should be $3/4$ of an inch longer. When the design is finalized, it's ready to go into production. It can then be

## INCLUSIVE FASHION

Fashion comes in all sizes—and fashion designers do, too. Just ask Egypt Ufele of Queens, New York. In February 2016, Egypt showed her line of clothing at New York Fashion Week. Fashion Week is a huge event where top designers show off their latest designs. Egypt was just ten years old. She was chosen to participate in Fashion Week because she makes clothes for people with a range of body types, including plus-size fashions.

Egypt wears plus-size styles herself. She started creating her own designs after kids at her school bullied her. She always liked to sew. She was sewing dolls' clothes when she was five years old. Egypt has designed many items using African prints. She told The Huffington Post that she loves fashion because it can "make you feel good."

made in many sizes for customers.

When designers sketch their fashion creations, it's not practical for them to make life-sized drawings. They have to translate their ideas from small sheets of paper or screens into the actual size. To do that, they increase the scale, or size, of their designs by using ratios and multiplication.

For example, perhaps a designer has drawn a sketch for a dress at $^{1}/_{4}$ scale. That means that it's $^{1}/_{2}$ of life size. The relationship, or ratio, between the sketch and real life is 1:4. In order to arrive at the full-scale design pattern, the designer multiplies the drawing measurements by 4. When scaling up or down, you'll often work with fractions. To multiply with a mixed number, such as 2 $^{1}/_{3}$, convert it into an improper fraction. A whole number appears as the numerator equaling the denominator. $1 = {}^{3}/_{3}$; $2 = {}^{3}/_{3} + {}^{3}/_{3} = {}^{6}/_{3}$; $3 = {}^{3}/_{3} + {}^{3}/_{3} + {}^{3}/_{3} = {}^{9}/_{3}$; and so on. You must add those whole numbers to the remaining fraction. For 2 $^{1}/_{3}$, that looks like this: ${}^{3}/_{3} + {}^{3}/_{3} + {}^{1}/_{3} = {}^{7}/_{3}$.

A prototype like this allows the designer to see what the completed garment will look like when someone wears it. Prototypes reveal what adjustments may be necessary.

Once a pattern is finalized, scaling also creates the garment in different sizes. If the waist measurement for one size is 28 inches and the waist measurement for the next larger size will be 30 inches, all of the pattern pieces are scaled up so they'll fit together correctly in the larger size.

## TECHNOLOGY ADDS A NEW DIMENSION TO FASHION

As designers use computers in creating designs, consumers can use technology to determine which size to buy. One type of computer program, often called a virtual fitting room, collects a customer's body measurements with a scanner. Sometimes the scanning is done at a special booth in a store. The program takes the scanned images and creates a three-dimensional avatar, or virtual mannequin. This helps customers determine their proper clothing size faster than doing all their measurements with a tape measure. Some programs, or apps, allow customers to do the scanning at home. They can use the camera on a laptop or phone to make three-dimensional images of themselves. The computer app identifies measurement points,

### TRY IT YOURSELF

A designer at Hillary House sketched a design for a silk jacket. On the drawing, the jacket sleeves are 3 inches long. The actual arm length for sleeves will be 21 inches. The drawing shows the front length of the jacket is 2 ½ inches.

5a. What will the length of the front of the finished jacket be?

A loom holds many threads that are woven together to make cloth. A Jacquard loom *(pictured)* can be programmed to weave designs such as leaves or vines into the fabric.

such as height, shoulder width, and waist size, and matches those to the correct clothing sizes. With some programs, users input their own weight, which is incorporated into the computerized size calculation. It's high-tech fashion!

In fact, the fashion industry has been using cutting-edge technology for centuries. In 1801, cloth-making factories utilized automatic programs to weave different-patterned fabrics. The Jacquard loom, first used in France, was programmed using special cards with holes punched into them. These cards controlled the threads as they were woven to make flower patterns or other designs in the cloth. When early computers were invented, similar punch cards transmitted their instructions, or programs, to tell the computers what to do. It gives a new meaning to "fashion forward!"

CHAPTER 6

# Making Money in the Fashion Business: Costs, Prices, and Profit

Success in the fashion trade requires artistic vision plus business sense. Many fashion designers start their own companies or work on their own. To make a living in the world of fashion requires a good working knowledge of costs, prices, and profit.

## HOW MUCH DOES IT COST?

You've probably noticed that there is a large range of prices in clothing stores. The price you pay for an item depends on many factors. One major factor is the cost of production.

People selling clothing must decide how much to charge for an item in order to make enough money to stay in business. The person (or company) making the product sets a price when selling it to a retail store. Then the store must determine the price it will charge its customers. The seller will want to set prices that let it stay in business. That means the product should bring in enough money to cover the costs of making it, delivering it to the store or the customer, and other costs, such as advertising, with enough money left over for the seller to make a living. The costs of production include the materials plus the wages of the workers who made the item.

The prices of the jackets in this store are affected by factors such as the costs of distribution and overhead.

Let's say you designed a new style of jeans. You created a prototype and gave some samples to your friends. They tell you these are the most comfortable jeans they've ever worn and they look great, too. Now you want to try selling some of your great jeans.

To decide how much to charge, you'd start by adding up the costs of materials for a pair of jeans. You might have paid $10.00 for denim, $5.00 for a zipper, and $3.00 for a snap button. That's $18.00 in materials.

Then you'd consider labor costs. Say you hired someone who makes one pair of jeans in one hour, and you pay that person $20.00 per hour. That adds $20.00 to the cost of a pair of jeans. If you sewed the jeans yourself, you'd want payment for the value of your time, too.

The profit that a business makes is basically the difference between the costs of making a product and the money that the product brings in. It's not always easy to make a profit.

## TRY IT YOURSELF

Cali's Cute Clothing Company (Cali's) receives an order from a department store for 300 skirts in an assortment of sizes and colors. The store will pay Cali's $24.50 per skirt. The materials required to produce one skirt are listed on this table:

| Item | Cost (dollars) |
|---|---|
| Fabric | 9.50 |
| Buttons | 1.75 |
| Zipper | 4.25 |
| Lace trim | 1.25 |

The workers sewing the skirts can complete an average of three skirts per hour. They receive $15.75 per hour.

6a. What is the total amount that Cali's will receive for this order?

6b. What profit will Cali's make on this sale?

# BUT WAIT, THERE'S MORE!

There are considerations other than costs of materials and labor that affect a business's profit. For example, a fashion designer might pay rent for a design studio or a retail store space. Or a company may pay a certain number of employees regardless of how much business it's doing. This category of costs is called overhead, or fixed costs. A business needs to bring in enough money to cover its overhead.

Consider Valentina, a fashion designer who made sales of $40,000 in her first year in business on her own. Her costs for materials and labor were $30,000. But Valentina did not make a profit of $10,000 because she also had to pay an annual rent of $9,600. As a result, in her first year she made just $400 more than the costs of her business.

Smart businesspeople also invest in their business. For example, Anjana wants to buy 50 new sewing machines in order to produce her clothing more quickly. When making investments like these, businesspeople consider the return they expect on their investment. She has calculated that she'll make $500 per month more in sales due to their increased speed. The banker will consider this information in determining whether it's a good investment to loan the money Anjana needs to buy the machines.

Workers in large factories sew garments for buyers around the world. Clothing manufacturers set their prices based in part on the wages paid to the people making the clothes.

Education is an investment, too. Darnell, who wants to be a fashion designer, believes going to design school will improve the quality of his designs and help move his career forward. Wherever he goes to school, Darnell will pay attention in math class because he knows math skills are mandatory for design and business in the fashion industry.

# Answers

Answer 1a. To take 25 percent off of the $40 price, Sam first calculates 25 percent of $40.00 by multiplying the price by 0.25.

$40.00 • 0.25 = $10.00. So Sam can take $10.00 off the regular price. That's $40.00 – $10.00 = $30.00.

He knows that $50.00 – $30.00 = $20.00, so if he buys these jeans, he'll have $20.00 left.

Answer 1b. The shirts are normally priced at $22.50, but the first shelf of on-sale shirts looks like a bargain. Half off of $22.50 is just $11.25.

$\frac{1}{2}$ • $22.50 = $22.50 ÷ 2 = $11.25

But there's a problem. To receive this discount, Sam must first buy one shirt at full price, $22.50. That's over his budget even before he adds the shirt that would be half off.

Sam turns to the second shelf, where he can get a shirt for $5.00 off the regular price. Since they're regularly $22.50, the following demonstrates that he can buy one: $22.50 – $5.00 = $17.50. His remaining cash, $20.00, is more than $17.50, so he has enough to buy jeans and a shirt.

Answer 1c. Overall, he'll spend $30.00 on jeans plus $17.50 on a shirt, for a total of $47.50. The amount of cash he has minus the total cost of the jeans and shirt leaves him with a few dollars and some change: $50.00 – $47.50 = $2.50.

*Tax note:* In some places, the customer pays a local sales tax, which is added to the price of goods. For example, if the sales tax is 5 percent, on a $10.00 item, the customer pays 50 cents in tax for a total of $10.50. Tax rates vary. In New Hampshire, for instance, there's no sales tax, while New York City charges no sales tax on clothing priced under $110. Before taking your loot to the cash register, know your local sales tax rate.

Answer 2a. Take the current length of 17 $\frac{3}{4}$in and subtract Ame's target length of 14 $\frac{1}{2}$in. To do this, convert the $\frac{1}{2}$ to the equivalent fraction $^{2}/_{4}$. This allows you to subtract two fractions with the same denominator: 17 $^{3}/_{4}$ in – 14 $^{2}/_{4}$ in = 3 $^{1}/_{4}$ in.

Answer 2b. One way to calculate this is to take the final length she wants (14 $^{1}/_{2}$ in) and add the depth of the hem (1 $^{1}/_{4}$ in). Again, convert the $^{1}/_{2}$ to the equivalent fraction $^{2}/_{4}$. Thus, 14 $^{2}/_{4}$ in + 1 $^{1}/_{4}$ in = 15 $^{3}/_{4}$ in. The skirt is currently 17 $^{3}/_{4}$ in long. Subtract 15 $^{3}/_{4}$ in to determine how much to cut off. Thus, 17 $^{3}/_{4}$ in – 15 $^{3}/_{4}$ in = 2 in.
Ame should cut off 2 in of fabric at the bottom.

Answer 3a. Using the formula $V = L \cdot W \cdot H$, the result is 14 in • 12 in • 4 in = 672 in$^3$. Don't forget to label the units!

Answer 4a. To figure this out, Sondra converts all the measurements to feet. The cloth she wants to buy is 60 in wide. Since there are 12 in for each foot, dividing these two values describes the length of the fabric in feet: 60 ÷ 12 = 5. The fabric is 5 ft wide.
Since 1 yard equals 3 ft, if Sondra buys a length of 1 yard of fabric, she'll have a rectangular piece that is 5 ft by 3 ft.
Sondra uses the formula $A = L \cdot W$, substituting 5 ft for the length and 3 ft for the width, and the result is 15 ft$^2$. This means if Sondra buys 1 yard, she'll have 15 ft$^2$ of fabric. To get 30 ft$^2$, Sondra must double that amount and purchase 2 yards. So, Sondra should buy 2 yards of fabric.

Answer 5a. To convert the measurements in the drawing to the actual dimensions of the jacket, the designer must know the relationship, or ratio, between the drawing and the full-scale garment.
If the 3-in sleeves on the drawing will be 21 in when life-sized, the scale is 3/21. That ratio, or fraction, can be simplified to $^{1}/_{7}$.
Thus, the ratio between the drawing and the full-scale garment is 1:7. That means that to convert from the measurements of the

drawing to the real-life measurements, you multiply by 7.

To do so, you'd look to the 2 $\frac{1}{2}$-in length on the drawing. Start by converting 2 $\frac{1}{2}$ in to an improper fraction, $\frac{5}{2}$ in, to aid in multiplication. From there, multiply and reduce: $7 \cdot \frac{5}{2}$ in = $\frac{35}{2}$ in = 17 $\frac{1}{2}$ in.

Answer 6a. Multiply the cost of each skirt by the total number of skirts Cali's is selling: $24.50 • 300 = $7,350.00. This is the amount Cali's will earn from the sale.

Answer 6b. To determine the profit, first figure out the material costs. Then determine the labor costs.

The chart shows the costs of materials. Add to determine the cost of materials to make one skirt: $9.50 + 1.75 + 4.25 + 1.25 = $16.75.

The material cost for 300 skirts would be $16.75 • 300 = $5,025.

If a worker can make three skirts per hour, that's three skirts for $15.75. To derive the labor cost of one skirt, divide $15.75 by 3: $15.75 ÷ 3 = $5.25.

The labor costs for 300 skirts is: $5.25 • 300 = $1,575.00.

The material and labor costs together are: $5,025.00 + $1,575.00 = $6,600.

The total amount received for the order, minus the costs, is the profit: $7,350 – $6,600 = $750.00.

# GLOSSARY

**ALTERATION** A change in a piece of clothing, especially to improve the fit.

**AREA** The amount of space within the boundary of a flat, or two-dimensional, shape such as a rectangle or circle.

**BUDGET** A fixed amount of money available to spend.

**CONVERT** To change or translate from one form or system to another.

**DENOMINATOR** The number below the line in a written fraction.

**DIMENSIONS** The measurements of an object, such as length, width, and height.

**DISCOUNT** A reduction in price.

**GARMENT** An item of clothing.

**GEOMETRY** A branch of mathematics concerned with the properties of lines and shapes.

**HEM** The edge of a pair of pants, a skirt, or other garment where the fabric is usually turned under and sewed down.

**INSEAM** The line of sewing running inside the leg of a pair of pants from the hem to the crotch, or the measurement of this line.

**INVEST** To put money into a business with the expectation of earning money from that business's profits.

**MANNEQUIN** A dummy, or model of a person, used to display clothing.

**MEASURING TAPE** A ruler made of cloth or other flexible material marked with inches and/or centimeters used to measure nonflat objects.

**OVERHEAD** The fixed costs of running a business, including rent and furniture, that are not impacted by the amount of a good that is made.

**PATTERN** A plan for sewing that includes diagrams of the shapes to be cut out of fabric and sewn into a garment.

**PERCENTAGE** A quantity expressed as parts per 100.

**PROFIT** The amount of money made in the sale of an item after accounting for the costs of producing the item.

**PROPORTION** The relationship of the size or shape of one thing to another or between parts of a whole.

**PROTOTYPE** A model of a new design, such as a clothing sample.

**RATIO** The relationship in size or quantity between two values.

**RECTANGULAR PRISM** A three-dimensional object that has six faces that are all rectangles.

**SCALE** The proportion between an object's original size or quantity and the object re-created in a form that is of greater, lesser, or the exact same size or quantity.

**THRIFT STORE** A shop that sells secondhand, or used, clothing and other goods.

**VOLUME** The amount of space that a three-dimensional object takes up measured in cubic units.

# For More Information

Association of Sewing and Design Professionals
2885 Sanford Avenue SW, #19588
Grandville, MI 49418
(877) 755-0303
Website: http://www.sewingprofessionals.org
This organization focuses on education and networking for individuals in sewing and design businesses. It supports students in fashion design by holding a design challenge and encourages student attendance at the organization's national educational conference.

Canadian Mathematical Society
209-1725 St. Laurent Boulevard
Ottawa, ON K1G 3V4
Canada
(613) 733-2662
Website: http://cms.math.ca
The society promotes and celebrates mathematics and supports math education in Canada. It sponsors national mathematics competitions and trains students to participate in them.

Costume Museum of Canada
301-250 McDermot Avenue
Winnipeg, MB R3B OS5
Canada
(204) 989-0072
Website: http://www.costumemuseumcanada.com
This is Canada's first museum to specialize in clothing and textiles. It has a substantial collection of costumes, clothes, and

accessories and offers public programs.

Math Counts Foundation
1420 King Street
Alexandria, VA 22314
(703) 299-9006
Website: https://www.mathcounts.org
This organization works to get middle school students excited about math by offering an engaging competition series and a nationwide math club, and it encourages students to create an educational math video.

Mathematical Association of America
1529 18th Street NW
Washington, DC 20036-1358
(800) 741-9415
Website: http://www.maa.org
The association welcomes all who are interested in mathematics. It supports math education and encourages students to pursue activities and careers related to math.

## WEBSITES

Because of the changing nature of Internet links, Rosen Publishing has developed an online list of websites related to the subject of this book. This site is updated regularly. Please use this link to access this list:

http://www.rosenlinks.com/MYWAU/fashion

# For Further Reading


Albee, Sarah and Tim Gunn. *Why'd They Wear That? Fashion as the Mirror of History*. Washington, DC: National Geographic, 2015.

Andrus, Aubre. *Math + Fashion = Fun: Move to the Head of the Class with Math Puzzles to Help You Pass!* Middleton, WI: American Girl Publishing, 2012.

Culp, Jennifer. *Cosplay* (Role-Playing for Fun and Profit). New York, NY: Rosen Publishing Group, 2016.

Dallas, Justin. *Fashion Photographer* (The Coolest Jobs on the Planet). Chicago: Raintree, 2015.

Fontichiaro, Kristin. *Hacking Fashion: Fleece*. Ann Arbor, MI: Cherry Lake Publishing, 2016.

Kuskowski, Alex. *Cool Refashioned T-shirts: Fun & Easy Fashion*. Minneapolis, MN: Checkerboard Library, an imprint of Abdo Publishing, 2016.

Levete, Sarah. *Maker Projects for Kids Who Love Fashion* (Be a Maker!). New York, NY: Crabtree Publishing Co., 2016.

Lisle, Andria, and Amie Petronis Plumley. *Sewing School: 21 Sewing Projects Kids Will Love to Make*. Pownal, VT: Storey Publishing, 2015.

Simons, Rae. *Fashion Math*. Broomall, PA: Mason Crest, 2014.

Taylor, Chloe. *Ready to Wear*. New York, NY: Simon Spotlight, 2013.

Worth, Richard. *Vera Wang: Fashion Designer* (Influential Asians). New York, NY: Enslow Publishing, 2016.

# BIBLIOGRAPHY


Bazley, Tarek. "3D Body Scanning Set to Disrupt Clothing Industry." Al Jazeera English, September 3, 2015. http://www.aljazeera.com/news/2015/09/3d-body-scanning-set-disrupt-clothing-industry-150903112712046.html.

Carlozo, Lou. "$50 for a T-shirt? Please. Thrift Shopping Saves You 50% to 80% on Clothes." Deal News, August 22, 2013. http://dealnews.com/features/50-for-a-T-Shirt-Please.-Thrift-Shopping-Saves-You-50-to-80-on-Clothes/827487.html.

Cornell University, College of Human Ecology. "Made-to-Measure." Retrieved September 30, 2016. http://www.bodyscan.human.cornell.edu/scenefe80.html.

Feldman, Jamie. "5th-Grader Bullied By Her Classmates Debuts Clothing Line at Fashion Week." Huffington Post, February 18, 2016. http://www.huffingtonpost.com/entry/5th-grade-fashion-designer_us_56c4bc56e4b0c3c55053614d.

Grant, Linda. *The Thoughtful Dresser: The Art of Adornment, the Pleasures of Shopping, and Why Clothes Matter*. New York, NY: Scribner, 2009.

Laing, Laura. "Math at Work Monday: Sole the Fashion Designer." Math for Grownups, December 17, 2012. http://mathforgrownups.com/math-at-work-monday-sole-the-fashion-designer.

Menkes, Suzy. "Designers Outline a New Geometry." *New York Times*, March 5, 2010. http://www.nytimes.com/2010/03/06/fashion/06iht-rrick.html?_r=0.

Nicolay, Megan. *Beyond Fashion: 120 New Ways to Transform a T-shirt*. New York, NY: Workman Publishing, 2009.

Riccio, John. "Virtual Dressing Rooms Will Become Reality Sooner than You Imagined." PWC Digital Pulse, July 27, 2015. https://www.digitalpulse.pwc.com.au/virtual-dressing-rooms.

Romano, Lauren. "How Does Math Work in Fashion Everyday?" eHow. Retrieved August 24, 2016. http://www.ehow.com/facts_5531772_math-work-fashion-everyday.html.

Shaeffer, Claire B. *Couture Sewing Techniques*. Newtown, CT: The Taunton Press, 2007.

Strongman, Luke. "Force Field: Vitruvian Man and the Physics of Sensory Perception." *International Journal of Arts and Sciences*, 2010. http://citeseerx.ist.psu.edu/viewdoc/download?doi=10.1.1.301.9649&rep=rep1&type=pd.

Symonds, Alexandria. "Mixing Math With Fashion." *Wall Street Journal*, February 5, 2013. http://www.wsj.com/articles/SB10001424127887323807004578286370689853666.

Thomas, Rachel. "Career Interview: Fashion Designer." *Plus*, December 1, 2009. https://plus.maths.org/content/career-interview-fashion-designer.

Wolfe, Jonathan. "Rulers and Runways." *New York Times*, September 8, 2016. http://www.nytimes.com/2016/09/08/nyregion/new-york-today-public-school-fashion-week-start.html?_r=0.

# INDEX


## A

advertising, 8, 33
alteration, 4, 10, 12–13
area, 16, 23
avatar, 30

## B

budget, 5–7, 9

## C

clothing swap, 7
convert, 14, 21–23, 25–26, 29
cost, 4, 9, 32–35

## D

Deal News, 8
denominator, 29
dimensions, 12–16, 18–19, 28, 30
discount, 5–9
DIY (do it yourself), 21
dress, 13, 25, 29

## E

emergency alterations, 13

## F

fixed costs, 34

## G

garment, 5–6, 12–13, 16, 23–25, 27–29, 35
geometry, 4, 15, 17

## H

height, 16–17, 20, 31
hem, 12–14
Huffington Post, The, 28

## I

improper fraction, 29
inseam, 11

## J

Jacquard loom, 31

## L

labor, 33–35
length, 14, 16, 20, 23, 25–26, 28, 30
Leonardo da Vinci, 17

## M

mannequin, 20, 28, 30
materials, 24, 26, 33–35
measuring tape, 5, 10, 21–22
metric system, 21–22
mixed number, 29

# Index


## N

New York Fashion Week, 28

## O

online shopping, 7–8, 14
overhead, 33–34

## P

pattern, 4, 23–24, 28–30
percentage, 6, 8–9
plus size, 13, 28
price, 4–10, 32–33, 35
profit, 32–35
*Project Runway*, 4
proportion, 4, 17, 20, 28
prototype, 27–28, 33

## Q

quality, 8, 35

## R

ratio, 4, 27, 29
rectangular prism, 18–19
rent, 34–35
resale store, 7, 8
return policies, 9

## S

sales, 5–7, 9, 12, 34–35
scale, 27, 29–30
school, 6, 28, 35
shipping, 9
size, 4–5, 9–14, 16–18, 21, 24, 27–31, 34
sizing systems, 10, 13

## T

thrift stores, 8

## U

Ufele, Egypt, 28
United States customary system, 21–22

## V

virtual fitting room, 30
Vitruvian Man, The, 17
volume, 4, 16, 18–19

## W

waist, 11, 13, 29–31
whole number, 29
width, 16, 20, 24–25, 31

# ABOUT THE AUTHOR

Christy Mihaly writes nonfiction for readers of all ages. She has written about math, science, technology, nature, and history. In her 2017 Rosen YA title *Getting Paid to Make Cosplay Costumes and Props*, she explored career possibilities arising from costume creation. During middle school and high school, Mihaly enjoyed sewing her own clothes. She has since then made clothing and costumes for various family members, including (just once) the dog. Her daughters may now disagree with her fashion sense, but they still let her help with measurements and clothing alterations. Mihaly's favorite math subject is geometry.

# PHOTO CREDITS

Cover, p. 1 Hero Images/Getty Images; p. 5 Manintino/iStock/Thinkstock; p. 6 Digital Vision/Photodisc/Thinkstock; p. 7 Image Source/Getty Images; p. 12 Petrovic Igor/Shutterstock.com; p. 14 Dreamcat/Shutterstock.com; p. 16 Matahiasek/Shutterstock.com; p. 17 Digital King/iStock/Thinkstock; p. 18 kali9/ E+/ Getty Images; p. 22 PhotographyFirm/iStock/Thinkstock; p. 23 Sofie Delauw/ Cultura/Getty Images; p. 26 Rosemary Calvert/Stockbyte/Getty Images; p. 29 Erstudiostok/iStock/Thinkstock; p. 31 Dennis K. Johnson/Lonely Planet Images/Getty Images; p. 33 Sabah Arar/AFP/Getty Images; p. 35 Christopher Pillitz/Photonica World/Getty Images; interior pages background Marina Sun/ Shutterstock.com.

Designer: Brian Garvey; Layout Designer: Greg Tucker; Editor: Bernadette Davis; Photo Researcher: Sherri Jackson